I DID IT HIS WAY

Johnny Hart

I DID IT HIS WAY

A collection of B.C. Religious comic strips

Johnny Hart

THOMAS NELSON
Since 1798

NASHVILLE   DALLAS   MEXICO CITY   RIO DE JANEIRO   BEIJING

I DID IT HIS WAY

Published in Nashville, Tennessee, by Thomas Nelson®. Thomas Nelson is a registered trademark of Thomas Nelson, Inc.

Thomas Nelson, Inc. titles may be purchased in bulk for educational, business, fund-raising, or sale promotional use. For information, please e-mail SpecialMarkets@ThomasNelson.com.

Unless otherwise noted, all scripture references are fom the HOLY BIBLE NEW INTERNATIONAL VERSION®. © 1973, 1978, 1984 International Bible Society. Used by permission of Zondervan. All rights reserved.

Other scripture is taken from the NEW KING JAMES VERSION © 1979, 19780, 1982, 1992, Thomas Nelson, Inc.

Project Editor: Ariel Faulkner

ISBN 978-1-4041-8739-9

Printed and bound in China

09 10 11 12 [RRD] 5 4 3 2

www.thomasnelson.com

This book is dedicated to Johnny Hart and his many loyal fans of faith.

To our Johnny—husband, dad, and grandfather—
"May you walk with God." We love and miss you.

FOREWORD

From Johnny's wife, Bobby Hart:

Johnny and I envisioned this book for many years after he began writing inspirational strips for the *B.C.* series. When John passed on to heaven I knew I had to see our dream to completion. Now, with God's help we have done it both His, and John's way.

I would also like to express my gratitude to my friends and family, especially Perri, who has been so dedicated to this project, and Nancy, who first suggested the title. Thank you!

I pray you enjoy our dream.

Bobby Hart

"About the Beginning"

1950s, New York State.

Sitting at a desk in the art department of General Electric, a young man scribbles down an idea before returning to his work. By day, he is a dutiful employee, by night, a freelance cartoonist . . .

Johnny Hart had always been artistic, but he never considered that his idle sketches and clever jokes might lead to a legitimate career. Some might call it fate, others, Providence, but something led him to spend his life bringing laughter into the world.

Intrigued by the whimsical and informal style of the *Peanuts* comic he saw in the local paper every day, Johnny set out to create his own strip. He looked to the simple life of the prehistoric caveman for his inspiration, and soon the characters that were destined for fame began to emerge.

There was B.C. himself, a humble, naïve slob; Wiley, a superstitious poet with an aversion to water and a passion for sports; Cute Chick, the first pretty woman in a world that had not yet discovered objectivity; Curls, a master of sarcastic wit; Peter, a self-styled genius and the world's first philosophical failure; Clumsy Carp, a friendly, unassuming, narrow-minded klutz with an interest in ichthyology; Fat Broad, a gal with blunt honesty and an unswerving devotion to the domination of men; Thor, an inventor, artist, and self-proclaimed ladies' man; and Grog, a real caveman's caveman.

After signing with *The New York Herald Tribune* for

syndication, *B.C.* made its debut on February 17, 1958. The world of cartoons, and the twenty-seven-year-old Johnny, would never be the same. Johnny went on to become one of four cartoonists in history to have two comic strips picked up by over 1000 papers.

Over the years, *B.C.* has charmed audiences of all ages and walks of life. When Johnny became a Christian in 1984, he was called to put his art to work for the Lord. His new-found faith began to appear in his comics, varying from light-hearted comedy to moving and thought-provoking content. Today, his family would like to share these inspirational strips as a tribute to Johnny's God-given talent and ever-lasting grace.

"Prayer is allowing God to have His will in your life on HIS terms."

—JOHNNY HART (1931-2007)

Johnny's favorite scripture

And Jesus answered them,

"Have faith in God."

MARK **11:22** AS WELL AS **11:23–24**, , AND JOHNNY SAYS, "LOOK IT UP."
HE ALSO NOTED IN HIS BIBLE, "IF YOU DON'T BELIEVE IT, DON'T ASK."

BUFFALO WINGS

birth

BC BY JOHNNY HART

CAN YOU TELL ME HOW TO GET TO THE SUPERBOWL?

FIRST OF ALL YOU'RE GONNA HAVE TO PUT ON SOME WEIGHT...

MEN,..I DON'T HAVE TO TELL YOU WHY WE'RE HERE TODAY...

COACH

THE IMPORTANT THING TO REMEMBER IS **HOW** YOU GOT THERE.

IT WAS DEDICATION, TEAMWORK AND ABOVE-ALL..TALENT!

1·24

COACH

FOR SOME OF YOU, THIS MAY BE THE ONLY SUPERBOWL YOU EVER TAKE PART IN...

SO BEFORE WE SUIT-UP, LET'S BOW OUR HEADS AND GIVE THANKS

...DEAR LORD,

THANKS FOR LETTING ME STAND HERE, YEAR AFTER YEAR AND REHEARSE THIS SAME FUTILE SPEECH

25

BC BY JOHNNY HART

IS GOD....

GOD **IS** IN CHARGE.
by Wiley

WHEN WE PRAY, DOES OUR GOD HEAR?

WHEN WE BELIEVE, WILL WE STILL FEAR?

12·2

WE PRAY FOR PEACE, DEAR GOD — ONE DAY,

FOR LOVED ONES WHO'VE BEEN SWEPT AWAY.

MAY THEY WALK WITH YOU NOW, HAND IN HAND,

MAY THEY WATCH WITH YOU NOW, O'ER THIS GREAT LAND.

WHEN WE PRAY TO GOD, HIS EARS <u>DO</u> HEAR!

AND WHEN WE BELIEVE, WE SHALL <u>NOT</u> FEAR!

26

THE BIRTH OF a COMIC STRIP

One day, as he was on his way to the dentist's office, Johnny spied an old barn beside the road. Between the windows of the barn hung a little sign, which read, "To be continued."

Johnny often said that some ideas came to him so fast he had to scramble to write them down, while others took long hours of struggle. His family would laugh, saying, "I guess the devil really doesn't want you to do that one."

"To be continued" was one of the ones that came easily. It was published on April 20, 2003.

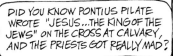
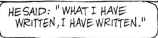

33

BC BY JOHNNY HART

EVEN THOUGH THE YEAST WAS CAST OUT OF THE DOUGH,

THE BREAD OF LIFE IS RISEN!

A MAN CALLED TRUTH TOLD ME ONE DAY, I MUST GO AWAY, FOR TO DIE.

©2006 CREATORS SYNDICATE, INC. www.creators.com

BUT AFTER 3 DAYS, I WILL COME BACK TO LIFE TO GO LIVE WITH MY DAD IN THE SKY.

4·16

NOW, IF YOU BELIEVE WHAT I TOLD YOU IS TRUE, I'LL GLADLY PREPARE A PLACE THERE FOR YOU...

YOU'D BUILD ME A PLACE JUST BECAUSE I BELIEVE? ...AND I'LL COME BACK TO TAKE YOU THERE, TOO!

—OR ANYONE ELSE YOU SHOULD CARE TO TELL, WHO WOULD LIKE TO GO THERE AS WELL. YOU'D MAKE THEM A PLACE AS WELL?

I AM A CARPENTER'S SON, YOU KNOW! I KNOW. YOU DO?—HOW DID YOU KNOW? BECAUSE THE BIBLE TOLD ME SO. —OH.

DID IT ALSO SAY, I WOULD PAY THE PRICE FOR YOUR SINS, AND DIE FOR YOU, TOO? —YES!

BUT, NOW YOU ARE RISEN! RISEN INDEED! NO LONGER DEAD! WHEN THE SON OF GOD SAYS, HE WILL COME BACK FOR YOU, HE MUST LIVE UP TO WHAT HE HAS SAID.

DEVOLUTION

A THEORY BY WHICH A DINOSAUR — GIVEN
ABOUT 300 BILLION YEARS, OF COURSE —
CAN RETROGRESS TO AN AMOEBA

steeplejack

MONEY RAISED FOR
THE NEW STEEPLE

36

BC BY JOHNNY HART

AMAZING! THE ONLY PLANET IN THE UNIVERSE WITH INTELLIGENT LIFE.

HEY, WHAT ABOUT US?

SIGH IT AIN'T EASY BEING GREEN.

GOD...

...YOU THERE?

ALWAYS.

YOUR MOON IS SO BEAUTIFUL!

THANKS.

BUT...

BUT WHAT?

HOW COME WE ONLY GET ONE MOON AND JUPITER GETS SIXTEEN?

EVER TRY TO LIGHT UP THE ASTRODOME WITH A 50-WATT BULB?

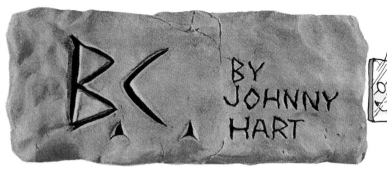

 GOT a DATE with an ANGEL ♫

 SQUISH

 SLAM

2·25

 WHOOPS! WHOOOOAAA

 YOU'RE 5 MINUTES LATE.

 IT'S GOD'S FAULT.

 YOU CAN'T JUST GO AROUND BLAMING GOD FOR YOUR OWN BLUNDERS.

 WHY NOT?...HE INVENTED THE LAW OF GRAVITY, DIDN'T HE?

IT'S NICE TO HAVE
A WOODEN LEG,

ON WHICH TO CRACK
AN EASTER EGG.

EASTER IS A TIME OF LOVE

A TIME THAT LETS US KNOW

WE HAVE A CHANCE
TO RISE ABOVE

THE BAD TIMES HERE BELOW.

EASTER IS
THE BLINDING LIGHT

THAT CHASES OUT
THE BLINDNESS

OF ALL THE HATE
THAT'S IN THE WORLD

AND FILLS IT IN WITH KINDNESS.

45

BC BY JOHNNY HART

it was a dark and stormy night

...SOUNDS LIKE SOMETHING A DOG WOULD WRITE.

I'D LIKE TO SUBMIT A MANUSCRIPT FOR PUBLICATION.

HAVE YOU SOLD BEFORE?

A FEW MYTHS AND A FABLE OR TWO.

ANY BIG NAME PUBLICATIONS?

PRETTY BIG.

HOW 'BOUT THE BIBLE, EVER SOLD A PIECE TO THE BIBLE?

OKAY,....WHERE ARE THE HIDDEN CAMERAS?

48

50

prime rib

EVE.

altercation

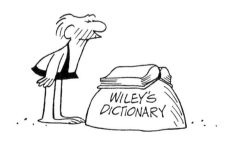

WHEN THE PREACHER
TAKES 2 WEEKS OFF.

Faith comes from hearing the message,
and the message is heard through the word of Christ.

ROMANS 10:17

B.C.
BY JOHNNY HART

WHAT'S THAT STAND FOR?

G.I.V.E.

ABOUT 5 BILLION BUCKS A YEAR.

G.I.V.E.

....BUT WITHOUT PRIVATE DONATIONS THEY COULD FALL ILL AND DIE AND ONE DAY THERE WOULD BE NO LITTLE BIRDIES TO SING

SOB! .....HERE'S MY LAST CLAM!

PLEASE, SIR?........ A CONTRIBUTION TO THE FIGHT AGAINST FALSE DECENCY?

...A.... ...SURE, WHY NOT....

A CONTRIBUTION TO THE BENEVOLENT FUND FOR UP-ENDED TURTLES?

...UH.....O.K.

3-26

WHAT'S WRONG WITH YOU?

I'M DESTITUTE!

HERE.

THE PRODIGAL CLAM, RETURNETH!

BY JOHNNY HART

WE'RE SO INFINITESIMAL WHY DOES THE WORLD HAVE TO BE SO HUGE?

OK...I GET IT.

WHO MADE THE CLOUDS, DAD?

GOD.

WHO MADE THE OCEANS AND THE MOUNTAINS?

GOD.

THE SAME GOD MADE THE BIRDS FLY AND THE GRASS GREEN?

YEP.

OKAY...WHAT ABOUT THE SUN AND THE MOON AND ALL THE STARS... WHO MADE THOSE?

GOD.

THERE'S NOTHING WRONG WITH DAD'S MIND, IS THERE, MOM?

OF COURSE NOT...

OH, SOMETIMES HE GETS HIS D'S AND G'S MIXED UP, BUT OTHER THAN THAT—HE'S FINE.

A DOG MADE ALL THIS?

57

58

59

60

BIBLE

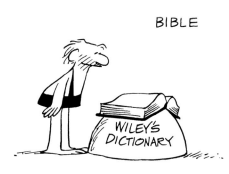

THE WORD FROM YOUR SPONSOR

WILEY'S DICTIONARY

2·5

GOOD FRIDAY

THE ONLY FRIDAY TRULY WORTHY OF THANKS TO GOD.

WILEY'S DICTIONARY

3·24

GOD LAID ON HIM, THE INIQUITY OF US ALL.

ISAIAH 53·6

AND HE FORGAVE US FROM THE CROSS, LUKE 23·34

...PAID THE RANSOM MARK 10·45

AND BOUGHT US AT A PRICE 1 COR. 6·20

FOR THE WAGES OF SIN, IS DEATH. ROM. 6·23

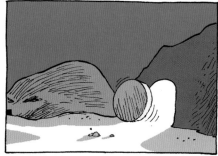

4·11

 TODAY, JOHNNY WILL RECITE HIS POEM ON FLAGS

 A FLAG IS JUST A PIECE OF CLOTH, VULNERABLE TO FIRE OR MOTH,

 YOU CAN HOIST IT WAY UP HIGH, AND WATCH IT FLAP AGAINST THE SKY

 YOU CAN MAKE IT ORANGE OR GREEN, OR ANY COLOR IN BETWEEN,

 WITH SHAPES LIKE HEXAGONS OR SQUARES, AND SOMETIMES LIONS OR EVEN BEARS.

 STARS AND STRIPES GET USED A LOTS, BUT SELDOM EVER, POLKA DOTS!

 THE COLORS I AM PARTIAL TO, SEEMS TO BE RED, WHITE, AND BLUE.

 THE WHITE FOR RIGHT, THE BLUE FOR TRUE,

 THE RED: —BLOOD SHED, FOR ME AND YOU.

 OL' BETSY ROSS, SHE MUSTA KNEW.

CLINK

BC BY JOHNNY HART

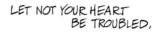
LET NOT YOUR HEART BE TROUBLED,

BELIEVE IN GOD, and ALSO IN ME.

" I AM THE WAY, THE TRUTH AND THE LIFE"

JOHN 14

—SAID THE MAN FROM GALILEE.

"I GO TO PREPARE A PLACE FOR YOU,

BELIEVE, AND YOU WILL SEE

THAT WHEN I AM THROUGH ,

©2005 CREATORS SYNDICATE, INC. www.creators.com

I WILL COME BACK FOR YOU,

3·27

SO THAT YOU MAY BE , WHERE I AM, TOO!

FOREVER —— YOU-and-ME."

68

THINGS I AM THANKFUL FOR:

I'M THANKFUL THAT I HAVE ONE LEG,

TO LIMP IS NO DISGRACE.

ALTHOUGH I CAN'T BE NUMBER ONE

I STILL CAN RUN THE RACE

IT'S NOT THE THINGS YOU CANNOT DO,

THAT MAKE YOU WHAT YOU ARE,

IT'S DOING GOOD WITH WHAT YOU'VE GOT

THAT LIGHTS 'THE MORNING STAR'

B.C. BY JOHNNY HART

NO PLAYOFF TODAY

I KNOW! I KNOW!

LAST PLACE AGAIN..... WHAT WENT WRONG?

I KNOW!....WE HAD LOUSY HITTING!

WAIT....WE LED THE ENTIRE LEAGUE IN R.B.I.'s....

9·28

THE PITCHING!...THAT WAS IT! **LOUSY PITCHING!**

NO,...WE POSTED THE LOWEST E.R.A. IN HISTORY......

THEN WHAT **WAS** IT? WHY ARE WE ALWAYS IN THE **CELLAR**?

DEAR GOD *SOB* GIVE ME A CLUE!

...SIX LETTER WORD FOR *Manager*, RHYMES WITH *Cupio*.....

OH, NOOOOoo

a Letter to God

In 1989, Johnny wrote a full week about the Cute Chick writing a letter to God despite Fat Broad's disbelief.

74

B C

BY JOHNNY HART

YOU FORGOT YOUR HOMEWORK, JOHN.

FEED IT TO THE APHID.

WHAT KEPT DANIEL FROM BEING EATEN ALIVE IN THE LION'S DEN?

SKOOL

9.21

JOHNNY?

HIS BIBLE.

HIS BIBLE?

HE READ TO THEM ALL NIGHT FROM HIS BIBLE.

THAT'S SO DARN <u>CUTE</u>, JOHNNY, I'M GOING TO ACCEPT IT!

ERGO...

ERGO?

ERGO, HE BECAME THE FIRST PROPHET, EVER, TO READ BETWEEN THE LIONS.

YOU GOT THROWN OUT OF RELIGIOUS CLASS?

GOD DON'T <u>REALLY</u> HATE PUNSTERS... DOES HE DAD?

FAST FOOD

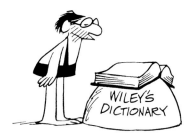

WHAT CATHOLICS CAN EAT FOR LENT.

IN·SIN·U·ATE

ADAM AND EVE'S LEAST FAVORITE WORD.

77

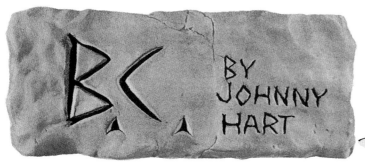

79

83

BC BY JOHNNY HART

TO BE......

OR ELSE.

OFTEN TIMES I WONDER WHAT THIS WORLD IS ALL ABOUT

IT CAN'T BE JUST A PLACE FOR COMING IN AND GOING OUT

IT SURELY CAN'T BE JUST A PLACE FOR TERRORISTS AND CROOKS..

AND DIRTY, ROTTEN SCOUNDRELS THAT SELL PORNOGRAPHIC BOOKS

IT WASN'T MADE FOR WALLOWING IN SICKNESS, DEATH AND SIN,

OR PEOPLE WHO GIVE DRUGS TO KIDS, OR BEAT-UP ON THEIR KIN.

12·10

OUR WORLD WAS ONCE A PERFECT PLACE, A GIFT OF LOVE, NOT WAR

AND WE STILL HAVE THE POWER, THROUGH GRACE, TO MAKE IT LIKE BEFORE!

hart

B.C. BY JOHNNY HART

WHAT CAME FIRST

THE RABBIT OR THE EGG....

WHAT IS THIS DAY ALL ABOUT?

HIDING EGGS FOR KIDS TO ROUT? CAKES AND COOKIES SHAPED LIKE LAMBS?

PINK CHAPEAUS ON PINK MADAMS?

THAT'S NOT WHAT IT'S ALL ABOUT!

WHO GOT BURIED THEN GOT OUT?

LEAVING NO ONE ANY DOUBT,

"HE IS RISEN", HEAR THEM SHOUT!

THAT'S WHAT THIS DAY'S ALL ABOUT.

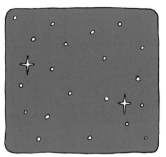

BC BY JOHNNY HART

TO WHOM IT MAY CONCERN,...

THAT WE MAY LIVE AND LEARN:

THE LAST WILL
AND TESTAMENT
OF GOD'S ONLY SON,

WAS A PROMISE THAT
YOU, ME, AND HE
WOULD BE ONE.

THAT HE WOULD BE WITH US
IN OUR DAILY LIFE,

TO CHASE ALL OUR WOES
AND TO BANISH OUR STRIFE.

HE WHO WAS PERFECT,
WHO NEVER KNEW SIN,

TOOK **OURS** TO HELL
SO THAT HE COULD GET IN!

...AND THAT'S HOW IT'S BEEN
SINCE HE TORE UP THAT PLACE,

JUST HE, YOU, AND ME,
SHARING GOD'S LOVING GRACE.

92

BULLY PULPIT

A PASTOR WHO THREATENS HIS CONGREGATION WITH A FOUR-HOUR SERMON

4·10

CROSS-REFERENCE

4·10

PSALM 22: 16-18

ISAIAH 53:5-7

REVELATION 1:7

Rejoice and be exceedingly glad,

for great is your reward in heaven. . . .

MATTHEW 5:12 NKJV

BY JOHNNY HART

REIGN TODAY

?

SPLAT

?

SPLAT

WHAT IN THE WORLD IS GOING ON?

IT'S PALM SUNDAY.

NICE GOING. HERE COME THE 'PUN POLICE'.

3-27

BC BY JOHNNY HART

WHAT TIME IS IT?

WRITE WRITE

by Johnny ant

AND NOW, CLASS, HEEEEEEEERE'S JOHNNY!

THERE IS A TIME FOR EVERY PURPOSE UNDER HEAVEN.

A TIME TO LAUGH, A TIME TO CRY, A TIME TO TRY APPEASIN'.

12-16

A TIME TO LIVE, A TIME TO DIE, "A REASON FOR THE SEASON."

A TIME FOR THE STRONG, A TIME FOR THE WEAK,

A TIME TO BE BOLD, A TIME TO BE MEEK,

A TIME FOR REFLECTION, A TIME FOR DOUBT, TO WONDER WHAT LIFE IS ALL ABOUT,

©2001 CREATORS SYNDICATE, INC. www.creators.com

A TIME TO SEEK AND THEN FIND OUT: IT'S GOD'S GOOD GRACE THAT FREES US,

TO KNOW THAT THE SEASON IS REALLY ABOUT —THE BLESSED BIRTH OF JESUS.

CLAP CLAP CLAP CLAP

AMEN

97

B.C.
BY JOHNNY HART

O "EVERGREEN TREE"
O "EVERGREEN TREE"

WHY DOEST THOU RHYME WITH 'ETERNITY'?

O CHRISTMAS TREE,
O CHRISTMAS TREE,
YOU BRING DELIGHT
AND JOY TO ME

©2005 CREATORS SYNDICATE, INC. www.creators.com

EACH YEAR I PLACE
UPON YOUR BREAST
THE STARRY HOST
WHICH GOD HAS BLESSED

ITS SHIMMERING LIGHTS
REFLECT THE CHEER
OF MEMORIES FROM YESTERYEAR

ON ORNAMENTS
THAT I REVERE
THAT TOUCH MY HEART
AND BRING A TEAR.

I PLACE THE STAR OF GRACE ON HIGH
TO WATCH ITS RADIANT GLOW,
FLOW DOWN THE STARRY HOST
AND REST UPON THE GIFTS BELOW

YOU—BETHLEHEM!
"THE HOUSE OF BREAD"
WHERE PROPHETS
SAID "HE SHALL BE BORN"

DID HOST INDEED, THE "WOMAN'S SEED,"
"THE BREAD OF LIFE" UPON THIS MORN.
IN HUMBLE STABLE, WRAPPED IN CLOTH
AND LAID INSIDE A FEEDING TROUGH,

12·25

"THE PRINCE OF PEACE"!
....WHO COULD FORESEE?
CAME TO US, AS
A CHRISTMAS TREE.
HAPPY BIRTHDAY, JESUS

102

RELIGIOUS CULT

THE CHURCH DOWN THE
STREET FROM YOURS.

pastoral scene

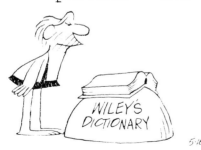

WHAT THE REVEREND
GOES THROUGH WHEN
HE COMES HOME LATE.

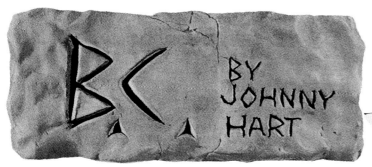

SOMETIMES CONTROVERSIAL

One of the most controversial *B.C.* strips that Johnny ever produced appeared on Sunday, April 15, 2001.

The power of the images he used made some believe that he was portraying the replacement of Judaism with Christianity, but Johnny was simply honoring two important holidays—Passover, represented by the menorah, and Easter, represented by the cross. The real thinking behind the strip was that Christianity is rooted in Judaism.

As Johnny explained, "I noticed one day that the center section of the menorah bore the shape of a cross. I wanted everyone to see the cross in the menorah. It was a revelation to me, one that tied God's chosen people to their spiritual next of kin—the disciples of the risen Christ. This was a holy week for both Christians and Jews alike, and my intent, as always, was to pay tribute to both."

Of the resulting hype, Johnny's wife, Bobby said, "When John began doing religious strips we knew there would be controversy. All he really wanted was for his readers to enjoy his work, look up Scriptures, maybe get a few laughs, and tell others about the message he prayed they would receive. Johnny never wrote a strip with the intention of offending anyone. That simply wasn't his nature."

THE BIBLE:
A BOOK OF SEVENS!
by Wiley

7 days
7 stars
7 loaves
7 vials
seven churches
7 seals
seven feasts

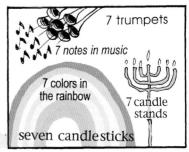

7 trumpets
7 notes in music
7 colors in the rainbow
7 candle stands
seven candlesticks

BC BY JOHNNY HART

THE SEVEN LAST 'WORDS' OF JESUS

Father, forgive them; for they know not what they do.

Verily I say unto thee, today you will be with Me in paradise.

TO THE THIEF | WHO KNEW

Woman, behold thy son! ... behold thy Mother!

TO MARY AND HER | NEW SON, JOHN

My God, my God, why hast thou forsaken me?

I thirst.

4/15

©2001 CREATORS SYNDICATE, INC. www.creators.com

Father, into thy hands I commend my spirit.

It is finished.

Do this in remembrance of me

115

the PROMISE

by Wiley

THE "Seed of the woman" WOULD COME ONE DAY

TO REMOVE THEIR SINS AND TO OPEN 'THE WAY.'

A PROPHET OF OLD HAD EVEN TOLD OF THE VERY DAY THAT HE WOULD COME

AND MANY TURNED OUT TO PRAISE AND SHOUT! THO' AMONG THEM— THERE WERE SOME

WHO EXPECTED A SAVIOR, WIELDING A SWORD,

IN PLACE OF A LOVING, COMPASSIONATE LORD.

BUT **HE** DIDN'T COME TO SAVE THEIR DAY, NOR THE HEAD OF ROME TO SEVER,

HE CAME TO DIE— TO BECOME "THE WAY," THE WAY TO LIVE —FOREVER.

118

E·PISTLE

NEW TESTAMENT VERSION OF E·MAIL

6·7

PAULBEARER

THE MAILMAN WHO DELIVERED THE
LETTERS TO THE ROMANS, CORINTHIANS,
GALATIANS, EPHESIANS, PHILIPPIANS,
COLOSSIANS AND THESSALONIANS

12·9

DARN...NOTHING RHYMES WITH GOSPEL — HOW CAN THAT BE POSSBLE?

HEY!

LISTEN UP, CLASS, JOHNNY HAS A POEM FOR US.

MARY HAD A LITTLE LAMB,

ITS FLEECE WAS WHITE AS SNOW

AND EVERYWHERE THAT MARY WENT

THE LAMB WAS SURE TO GO.

4·9

THEY JOURNEYED DOWN TO BETHLEHEM

TO SPEND A DAY OR TWO

AND WHEN THEY FOUND THE INN WAS FULL,

THE LAMB YELLED, déjà vu!

AMEN.

©2000 CREATORS SYNDICATE, INC. WWW.CREATORS.COM

120

124

125

IN OLDEN TIMES
LOST SOULS BESOUGHT

SWEET SOLACE
FROM THE GLOOM,

OF ALL THE SIN
THAT MAN HAD WROUGHT,

IN CONQUEST OF HIS DOOM,

AND THEN ONE NIGHT
A RAY OF HOPE

SHONE DOWN FROM
ONE BRIGHT STAR,

AND IN THAT MORN, A KING WAS BORN,

WHO LOVES US
AS WE ARE.

THE SUFFERING PRINCE

by Wiley

PICTURE YOURSELF
TIED TO A TREE,
CONDEMNED OF THE SINS
OF ETERNITY.

THEN PICTURE A SPEAR
PARTING THE AIR,
SEEKING YOUR HEART
TO END YOUR DESPAIR.

SUDDENLY—A KNIGHT,
IN ARMOR OF WHITE,
STANDS IN THE GAP
BETWIXT YOU AND ITS FLIGHT,

3.31

AND SHEDDING HIS
'ARMOR OF GOD' FOR YOU
—BEARS THE LANCE
THAT RUNS HIM THROUGH.

HIS HEART HAS BEEN PIERCED
THAT YOURS MAY BEAT,
AND THE BLOOD OF HIS CORPSE
WASHES YOUR FEET.

PICTURE YOURSELF
IN RAIMENT WHITE,
CLEANSED BY THE BLOOD
OF THE LIFELESS KNIGHT,

NEVER TO MOURN
THE PRINCE WHO WAS DOWNED,

FOR HE IS NOT LOST!
IT IS YOU
WHO ARE FOUND.

129

SAYS HERE JESUS MADE EVERYTHING THAT WAS MADE.

I DON'T BELIEVE IT.

WHY NOT? HE WAS A CARPENTER, WASN'T HE?

MAGNIFICENT!

AWESOME!

LET'S ALL MEET BACK HERE TOMORROW AT DAWN FOR A SUNRISE SERVICE!

GOOD IDEA! YES! ALL RIGHT! YEA! OKAY!

©2002 CREATORS SYNDICATE, INC. www.creators.com

ANYTHING WRONG, GROG?

GROG JUST THINKING.

3-31

OK, G'NITE.

SON RISE, SERVE US.

*SNIFF

133

A DAY IS... AS A THOUSAND YEARS.

by Wiley.

EVERYBODY DON'T ALL HAVE A FATHER.

SOME, THERE ARE, WHOSE DADS HAVE PASSED ALONG.

THEN THERE'S SOME WHO COULDN'T GIVE LESS BOTHER

6·15

TO FAMILY SITUATIONS WOEBEGONE.

WITH DADS YOU CANNOT JUST REACH OUT AND 'NAB' ONE

TO PULL THE FAMILY OUT OF ITS DESPAIR—

BUT IF FOR SOME REASON YOU DON'T HAVE ONE,

THERE'S ONE ON DUTY, ALL THE TIME —UP 'THERE'.

beatitudes

GOLD, FRANKINCENSE AND MYRRH

"This, then, is how you should pray:"
'Our Father in heaven, hallowed be your name. . .'

MATTHEW 6:9

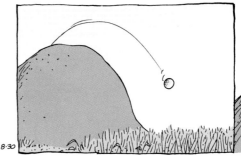

BC BY JOHNNY HART

STAR FAW DOWN.

SPLAT

SLING

GROG DO HIS PART TO GUIDE ALL MEN TO PEACE.

HAS ANYONE EVER PAINTED A PICTURE OF JESUS?

SURE. MANY ARTISTS. BUT NONE WHO EVER ACTUALLY SAW HIM.

THEN THAT MEANS NOBODY KNOWS WHAT HE LOOKS LIKE.

TRUE, BUT IT'S OKAY...

©2002 CREATORS SYNDICATE, INC. www.creators.com 12-22

I BELIEVE IT'S ALL PART OF GOD'S PLAN.

WHAT PLAN?

YOU KNOW—FAITH. "WE WALK BY FAITH, NOT BY SIGHT."

GEE... THAT'S GOOD! IS THAT FROM THE BIBLE?

YES.

STILL...

STILL, WHAT?

THERE'LL BE HELL TO PAY IN HEAVEN IF HE TURNS OUT TO BE A BIG BUNNY IN A SANTA CLAUS SUIT.

Hart
2 COR 5:7

WHO WAS THE EXECUTIVE PRODUCER FOR "THE GREATEST STORY EVER WRITTEN"?

TRIVIA TEST

10·3

ZOT

NO COACHING FROM THE AUDIENCE, PLEASE!

TRIVIA TEST

TO AVOID BAD PRESS, GENTLEMEN, I'M GOING TO BLAME OUR ROTTEN SEASON ON THE '7 DEADLY SINS'.

WHAT ARE THOSE?

7·27

PRIDE, LUST. ENVY, ANGER, COVETOUSNESS, GLUTTONY, SLOTH and NO RELIEF PITCHING.

THAT'S EIGHT!

...YOU'RE RIGHT.

SCRATCH PRIDE.

by Wiley

A SEED IS SUCH A MIRACULOUS THING,
IT CAN SIT ON A SHELF FOREVER.

BUT HOW IT KNOWS WHAT TO DO,
WHEN IT'S STUCK IN THE GROUND,
IS WHAT MAKES IT SO CLEVER.

IT DRAWS NUTRIENTS FROM THE SOIL
THROUGH ITS ROOTS,
AND GATHERS ITS FORCE FROM THE SUN.

IT PUTS FORTH A WHOLE LOT OF
BLOSSOMS AND FRUIT,
THEN RESEEDS ITSELF WHEN IT IS DONE.

WHO PROGRAMMED THE SEED TO
KNOW JUST WHAT TO DO?
AND WHO PUT THE SUN IN THE SKY?

AND WHO PUT THE FOOD IN THE
DIRT, FOR THE ROOTS?
AND WHO TOLD THE BEES TO COME BY?

AND WHO MAKES THE WATER
TO FALL FROM ABOVE,
TO REFRESH AND
MAKE EVERYTHING PURE?

PERHAPS ALL OF THIS IS A PRODUCT OF LOVE.
AND PERHAPS IT HAPPENED BY CHANCE.
YEAH, SURE.

145

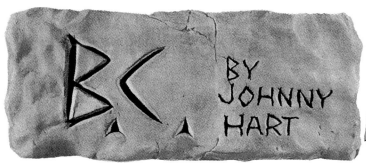

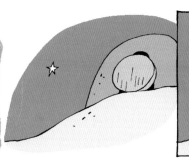

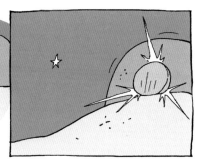

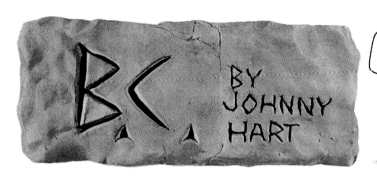

9·29

3·29

151

IT SEEMS TO ME THAT SINCE THE "FALL"

—WITHOUT EVEN THINKING IT ODD—

THAT MAN HAS HAD NO TROUBLE AT ALL

BELIEVING THAT HE CAN BE GOD.

HOW HE WOULD DO THIS I CANNOT CONCEIVE,

THO, HE CERTAINLY THINKS THAT HE CAN

—AND YET, HE CANNOT BRING HIMSELF TO BELIEVE,

THAT GOD CAN BECOME... A MAN.

©1997 CREATORS SYNDICATE, INC.

12·21

RECOLLECTION

WHEN THE USHER PASSES
THE PLATE AGAIN.

10·15

yuletide

THE TSUNAMI OF THE CHRIST

12·23

ODE TO A WAITRESS

$ 5.75

WHY DID GOD PUT WOMEN HERE ?

THEY'RE ALWAYS IN THE WAY!

THEY TELL US WHAT WE'RE S'POSED TO WEAR

AND WHAT WE'RE S'POSED TO SAY.

WHYEVER WOULD HE PUT THEM HERE,

TO AGGRAVATE AND TEASE US...?

I THOUGHT PERHAPS YOU'D LIKE A BEER .

GOOD GRIEF! THEY'RE HERE TO **PLEASE** US!

154

POOP DECK: slang

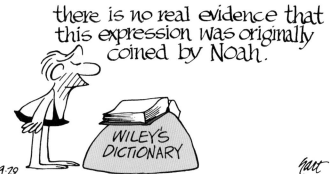

there is no real evidence that this expression was originally coined by Noah.

9·29

ADMINISTER

7·12

THE FINAL INGREDIENT IN A PAGAN, TRIBAL SOUP RECIPE.

157

BY
JOHNNY
HART

A CALENDAR IS FILLED WITH DAYS,
TO WHICH WE MUST ADHERE.

NO MATTER HOW YOU USE THEM,
THEY STILL ADD-UP TO A YEAR.

EACH MONTH WE CELEBRATE, WITH LOVE,
SOME VERY SPECIAL DAY,

THERE'S CHRISTMAS IN DECEMBER
AND MOTHER'S DAY IN MAY.

THO, FATHER'S DAY COMES 'ROUND IN JUNE,
HE LABORS IN SEPTEMBER

AND APRIL HAS A SPECIAL DATE
THAT ALL FOOLS WILL REMEMBER

WITH EACH JULY THE ROCKETS FLY
IN TEARFUL, PROUD RECALL

THEN 'AUGUST,' SO GRANDIOSE IN NAME,
HAS NO GOOD DAYS AT ALL!

NOVEMBER DOTH REMEMBER EVERY VETERAN,
WITH THANKSGIVING...

BUT BLESSED OF ALL IS EASTERTIME,
WHICH GIVES THE GIFT OF LIVING.

160

WAAAAAAAHH

ːSOBː

WHAT'S WRONG, SON?

WAAAAAH

SOBːALL THE KIDS AT SCHOOL MAKE FUN OF ME!

THEY SAY I LOOK STUPID!!...WAAAAHH

8·15

NONE OF US CAN HELP THE WAY WE LOOK, SON...

WHAT'S IMPORTANT IS HOW YOU FEEL INSIDE.

YOU **FEEL** INTELLIGENT DON'T YOU?

ːSNIFː YES....

THEN THERE YOU **ARE!** ...BESIDES,

..IF GOD HAD INTENDED FOR US TO LOOK **INTELLIGENT**, ...HE WOULDN'T HAVE GIVEN US 'DEELY BOBBERS'

WAAAAAAH!

hart

162

BC BY JOHNNY HART

THERE THEY GO WITH THEIR BIBLE.

YEP.

...MARY AND MARTHA.

ONE DAY, JESUS SUGGESTED TO SIMON PETER AND HIS FISHING PARTNERS THAT THEY PUSH OUT INTO THE DEEP WATER AND DROP THEIR NETS FOR A CATCH.

—AFTER TACTFULLY REMINDING JESUS THAT THEY HAD FISHED ALL NIGHT AND HAD CAUGHT <u>NOTHING</u>, PETER HUMORED HIS MASTER AND HONORED HIS REQUEST.

4·4

THEY CAUGHT SO MANY FISH THEIR NETS BEGAN TO BREAK, AND THEY CALLED OUT TO THEIR PARTNERS IN THE OTHER BOAT FOR HELP.

WHEN THEIR PARTNERS CAME, THEY FILLED BOTH BOATS SO FULL OF FISH THAT THEY BEGAN TO SINK!

SIMON PETER WAS ASHAMED, AND JAMES AND JOHN WERE AMAZED AND AWED!

"FEAR NOT," SAID JESUS, "FOLLOW ME, AND I WILL MAKE YOU FISHERS OF MEN." AND THEY IMMEDIATELY LEFT THEIR NETS AND FOLLOWED HIM.

WOW....WHAT A GUY—NO WONDER THEY FOLLOWED HIM!

YEAH.

...DIDN'T WANNA CLEAN THEM FISH.

164

MANGER

A FEEDING TROUGH LARGE ENOUGH TO CONTAIN 'THE BREAD OF LIFE'.

JOHN 6:35 hart

LIFE *n.*

ETERNITY 101

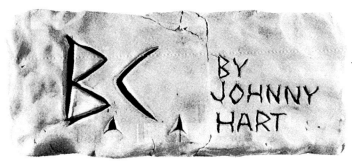

SHOWDOWN at the okie dokie CHORALE

by Wiley

HE RODE INTO TOWN
     PACKIN' A COLT,
AND THE TOWNFOLK
          CHEERED HIS WAY

AND HE STRODE UP BOLD
          TO THE TEMPLE FOLD
WHERE A ROWDY HORDE HELD SWAY.

HE KICKED THEIR CHAIRS,
     AND SEIZED THEIR WARE'S
AND THREW THEM
          DOWN IN THE DIRT!

THEN WHUPPED THEM
          UP ASIDE THE HEAD,
AND GAVE 'EM A TERRIBLE HURT.

THE LEGAL BROOD,
     IN A MANNER RUDE,
TOOK OFFENSE
          TO THE THINGS HE SAID,

IN A WAY, UNCOUTH,
     THEY SPURNED HIS TRUTH,
AND SOUGHT TO SEE HIM
               —DEAD

A TRAP OF LIES FOR HIS DEMISE,
THEY WOVE—
          AND THEY DREW HIM IN,

THEN, MUCH TO THEIR SURPRISE
     —HE SHED
     HIS BLOOD
          TO CLEANSE THEIR SIN.

STEEPLES MAKE FOR LOUSY ROOFS, THE RAIN JUST POURS RIGHT DOWN 'EM.

AUDACIOUSLY THEY STICK UP WAY PAST ALL THE ROOFS AROUN'EM.

JUST TO PAINT A STEEPLE WOULD REQUIRE AN ACROBAT.

STEEPLES HAVE NO FUNCTION 'CEPT TO POINT TO "WHERE IT'S AT."

173

JOHNNY'S FINAL STRIP

Sunday comics are written and produced approximately six weeks before their publication. On Easter Sunday 2007, the day after Johnny Hart passed away, this piece was printed. Ironically, it was the last inspirational *B.C.* comic strip he ever created.

BY JOHNNY HART

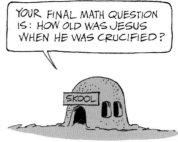

YOUR FINAL MATH QUESTION IS: HOW OLD WAS JESUS WHEN HE WAS CRUCIFIED?

SKOOL

YOU MAY TURN IN YOUR TEST PAPERS NOW.

SKOOL

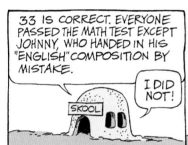

33 IS CORRECT. EVERYONE PASSED THE MATH TEST EXCEPT JOHNNY, WHO HANDED IN HIS "ENGLISH" COMPOSITION BY MISTAKE.

I DID NOT!

SKOOL

©2007 CREATORS SYNDICATE, INC.

THEN WHAT IS THIS?

IT'S A NUMERICAL DIALOGUE BETWEEN THREE PERSONS—

SKOOL

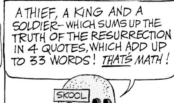

A THIEF, A KING AND A SOLDIER— WHICH SUMS UP THE TRUTH OF THE RESURRECTION IN 4 QUOTES, WHICH ADD UP TO 33 WORDS! *THAT'S MATH!*

SKOOL

OK, SMARTY PANTS, YOU READ, AND I'LL COUNT.

YES'M.

SKOOL

"JESUS, REMEMBER ME WHEN YOU COME INTO YOUR KINGDOM."

THAT'S NINE.

SKOOL

4-8

"ASSUREDLY I SAY TO YOU TODAY YOU WILL BE WITH ME IN PARADISE."

THAT'S 13.

SKOOL

"IT IS FINISHED."

"...TRULY THIS MAN WAS THE SON OF GOD."

SKOOL

WOW! 33 EXACTLY! ...WHAT CAN I SAY?

TRY AMEN PLUS.

SKOOL

177

This was found in Johnny's papers after his passing.
Written by Johnny, it has remained unpublished until now.

An unrecorded Psalm by David's son, Absalom

My bouffant hair was quite the fad
But much to my chagrin
When I rebelled against my Dad
My 'do' done did-me-in.

Johnny Hart— Awards for B.C.

- 1967 Best Humor Strip in America - The National Cartoonist Society

- 1968 The Reuben (Best American Cartoonist of the Year) - The National Cartoonist Society

- 1970 The Yellow Kid Award (Best Cartoonist of the Year) - The International Congress of Comics (Lucca, Italy)
  First-ever American recipient

- 1971 Best Cartoonist of the Year – (France)

- 1972 NASA Public Service Award (For outstanding contributions to NASA) - NASA
  Awarded for illustration of the Apollo 12 Flight Manual

- 1973 Best Animation Film Award - The National Cartoonist Society
  Awarded for "B.C. The First Thanksgiving"

- 1974 Silver Bell Award (Best Animated Television Commercial) - The Advertising Council
  Awarded for "B.C. Tickets for ACTION"

- 1974 Golden Spike Award (Best Animated Television Commercial) - The International Society of Radio and Television Broadcasters
  Awarded for "B.C. 'A' We're the ACTION Corps"

- 1976 "The Sam" Adamson Award (Best International Comic Strip Cartoonist) - The Swedish Academy of Comic Art

- 1981 The Elzie Segar Award (Outstanding Contributions to the Art of Cartooning) - King Features Syndicate

- 1982 Golden Sheaf Award (Special Jury Award) The Yorkton Short Film and Video Festival (Canada)
  Awarded for "B.C. A Special Christmas"

- 1982 Special Jury Award Outstanding Animation Overall - The Yorkton Short Film and Video Festival (Canada)
  Awarded for "B.C. A Special Christmas"

- 1986 Katie Award (Best Magazine Cover) - The Press Club of Dallas
  Awarded for cover illustration for "D Magazine"

- 1988 Telly Award (Best Television Commercial / Animation)
  Awarded for the animated commercial "Less filling" for the Monroe Shocks Corp.

- 1989 Best in the Newspaper, Strips, and Panels Category - National Cartoonist Society

- 1992 The Max and Moritz Award B.C. Best Comic Strip (Germany)

- 1995 Wilbur Award (Editorial Cartoon / Comic Strip Category) - The Religious Public Relations Council, Inc
  Awarded for Easter Sunday B.C. Strip 1995

- 2002 The Jefferson Award

About Johnny Hart

John Lewis "Johnny" Hart was born on February 18, 1931, in Endicott, New York. As a boy, he demonstrated a talent for art as well as an original sense of humor. "As far back as I can remember," he recalled, "I drew funny pictures, which got me out of, or into, trouble depending on the circumstances." But Johnny never considered cartooning as a serious profession until after he graduated from Union-Endicott High School in 1949, along with buddies Jack "Clumsy Carp" Caprio and Dick "Curls" Boland.

At age 19, Johnny met Brant Parker, a young cartoonist who influenced Johnny's artistic development and eventually became Johnny's creative partner for *The Wizard of Id* comic in 1964. Soon after his high school graduation, Johnny enlisted in the Air Force and was stationed in Warner Robins, Georgia. It was there that he met Ida Jane "Bobby" Hatcher. In 1952, Johnny and Bobby were married in the base chapel.

In 1953, Johnny was deployed to Korea, where he produced cartoons for the *Pacific Stars and Stripes*. After his discharge, the couple lived at his mother-in-law's farm in Georgia. It wasn't too long before Johnny sold his first freelance cartoon to *The Saturday Evening Post*.

Johnny returned to his hometown in New York State with his bride, and took a position in the art department at General Electric while continuing to sell cartoons to major magazines. Intrigued by the whimsical and informal style of the *Peanuts* comic he saw in the local paper every day, Johnny set out to create his own strip. He looked to the simple life of the prehistoric caveman for his inspiration, and soon the characters that were destined for fame began to emerge. *B.C.* signed with *The New York Herald Tribune* for syndication, and made its debut on February 17, 1958.

With his career as a cartoonist well under way, Johnny left his position at GE and began working full time on the strip. Johnny and Bobby were happy living in Endicott, raising their two daughters and enjoying *B.C.'s* success. In 1964, Johnny created a second comic strip, *The Wizard of Id*, with Brant Parker, his friend of fourteen years.

Producing two thriving comic strips was very rewarding, but coming up with funny ideas every day was challenging as well. Johnny found it particularly demanding in 1965 when his mother became very ill. Grace Hart lost her battle with cancer at the tender age of 53. Johnny

struggled with his grief and became very angry with God. He felt unable to accept this loss and needed answers that he could not find. Beyond the success of his professional life, he was struggling. In the years that followed, which Johnny later referred to as his "back-sliding years," he suffered from a lack of fulfillment in his life, and felt he might be drinking more than he should.

In 1976, a local realtor called Johnny to see if he might be interested in looking at a large wooded property in a neighboring rural town. Johnny fell in love with the peace and serenity of the place. It was a beautiful home surrounded by nature and set beside a pond. Unbeknownst to Bobby, he decided to purchase the property for her birthday and put it in her name. He knew she would love it as he did.

Oddly enough, the place was located in the small hamlet of Nineveh, New York. Johnny would later joke about how those who run away from God's purpose for them, like Jonah, get deposited in Nineveh sooner or later. After moving in, Johnny took up fishing and boating, and built a large studio on the property. Life seemed perfect. He had the career he had always dreamed of, and had become one of four cartoonists in history to have a two comic strips with over 1000 papers. He had a wife, children, and grandchildren who adored him, and a wonderful home. Yet something still seemed to be missing.

In 1984, Johnny decided he wanted better TV reception and called in a company to install a satellite dish at his studio. It became quite the operation and took longer than expected. A born-again father and son team owned the company Johnny had hired. They spent nights at the studio and used a Christian network to test the system. At first this annoyed Johnny, but he couldn't help but listen to the preachers on the station. To his astonishment, he was hearing that the Bible not only had all the answers he'd been searching for, it was *the* answer.

Johnny soon found his life taking on a new purpose and meaning. One Sunday morning he woke up and asked Bobby if she would like to go to church. Bobby didn't answer right away, so, Johnny began silently praying that she would want to go. The following Sunday she came to him and asked, "Do you want to go to that church?" Johnny smiled and together they began attending the Nineveh Presbyterian Church. They became members and made many new friends within the church family. Johnny began to gain an inner-peace and the profound knowledge that he was right with God.

His new-found faith called him to share the Word through his work. This decision was met with mixed reviews, which ranged from outright protest to enthusiastic applause. Although occasionally troubled by the debate, Johnny knew in his heart that this was God's purpose for his life.

Johnny would often recall one particular letter he received from a fan. A woman wrote to thank him. She had been seriously contemplating suicide, and happened to open the paper one day where she discovered one of his inspirational strips and it changed her life. Johnny said, "I couldn't believe it when I read that letter. God managed to use my strip to reach that precious soul." That one fan letter alone made all the controversy worthwhile.

Johnny's incredible wit and creative comic ability allowed him to reach the pinnacle of his profession. Lauded by his peers, he received numerous honors for both his comic strips, including the highest honor bestowed by the National Cartoonist Society, The Reuben. Although internationally famous, Johnny never forgot his roots, and freely donated his time and talent to his local community. Evidence of his generosity can still be seen all over Broome County, New York. From artwork to countless logos, including a PGA tour event, *"The B.C. Open,"* which ran for 35 years, Johnny has left his mark on the world. Measuring in at a mere 5 foot 6,

Johnny may have been small in stature, but he was big in "Hart."

God calls upon us to be good and faithful servants, and He found one of the best in Johnny Hart. That became evident on Easter eve 2007. God came to Johnny as he sat at his drawing board, doing what he loved, and peacefully took the man who had brought so much laughter into the world to be forever by His side.

Where do you go when you die?

To be absent
from the body is
to be present
with the Lord.

JH

B.C. by Johnny Hart

"You should know the truth,
and the truth shall make you free."

JOHN 8:32 NKJV

FROM JOHNNY'S DAUGHTER, PERRI:

I had once imagined working on this book with my dad, but now we have set out to do it *for* him, his way, or shall I say, HIS way!

I love and miss you Dad,

Perri

"TO BE CONTINUED"

Johnny Hart is survived by his wife, Bobby, two daughters, Patti and Perri, and two grandsons, Mason and Mick, who have all inherited his various talents. With Mason at the helm as *B.C.* artist, and Bobby guiding the way, the family is carrying on the tradition Johnny left behind. Everyone who loves *B.C.* can rest assured that the legacy will live on.

www.johnhartstudios.com